SOME THINGS
WORDS CAN DO

SOME THINGS
WORDS CAN DO

Martha Collins

The Sheep Meadow Press
Riverdale-on-Hudson, New York

All inquiries and permission requests should be addressed to:
The Sheep Meadow Press
PO Box 1345
Riverdale-on-Hudson, NY 10471

Designed by S.M.
Distributed by Unversity Press of New England.
Printed by McNaughton & Gunn, Inc.

Printed on acid-free paper in the United States. This book meets the guidelines for permanence and durability of the Committee on Production Guidelines for Book Longevity of the Council on Library Resources.

This book is published with the assistance of public funds from the Bronx Council on the Arts (BCA), through the Regional Arts Partnership Program of the Bronx Council on the Arts and the New York State Council on the Arts.

Library of Congress Cataloging-in-Publication Data

Collins, Martha
      Some things words can do / Martha Collins
            p.   cm.
      Includes A history of small life on a windy planet.
      ISBN 1-878818-74-0 (pbk. : acid-free paper)
      I. Collins, Martha.-   A history of small life on a windy
planet.   II. Title.
PS3553.04752S56   1998
811'.54—dc21
COLLINS
                                                                98-42844
                                                                      CIP

SOME THINGS WORDS CAN DO

for Myra Goldberg

and Jane Cooper

CONTENTS

SOME THINGS WORDS CAN DO

Play. Teach us
to play. Play for us.

Take us. Take us in.
Take us out. Introduce us.

Make something
of us. Make us ours.

Leave us. Leave
us wanting.

I

PINKS

If you wanted flesh you had to wait
till second grade, for the box
of 64. Until then you outlined us
in orange, or maybe filled us in,
but then we looked like Halloween.
You never used white, though white came
in the 16 box; it didn't show, and besides,
white was wrong: we looked like ghosts.
Of course you could use pink. But pink
was too pink, like flowers, or clothes.

*

To pink is to thrust is to pierce
(with a bullet), to scallop (with little
eyes) along the edge, as in (perhaps,
depending on dates) the flower behind
(most likely) the color.

*

Ascot   Carnea   Delicata
Lady Blanche   Harry Hooper   Mrs. Simkins
Attraction   Criterion   Reliance

*

Pink-cheeked pink-lipped
sea-pink shell-pink

At the turn
of the century pink
was the color for boys

*

You only used flesh
for flesh. It was wrong
even for flowers, which was where,
around the house, you could use
almost any color in the box.
It wasn't pink or peach.
It wasn't pretty.
It was skin.

*

Pink was what some of us got
in summer, which wasn't as good
as tan or brown, and browner
than even some Blacks was best,
though we didn't say Blacks
back then and of course
it was clear you really
weren't, though you might
have a touch of Indian
blood: my friend was related
to Pocahontas, who was better
than anyone anyone else could claim.

*

The library had, in its children's
section, stories of Young Americans
covered in orange. The illustrations
were silhouettes, i.e. the people
were black. But among the dozens
of orange books, there were only two
about Blacks. Most of the women
were Mothers and Wives; all
except Pocahontas were white.

*

George Washington Carver made
   the peanut (underground, tan)
the second largest crop in the South
   after cotton (aboveground, white).

*

white sheets pink blanket white
spread white curtains a dancing doll
in pink-white skirts to match the pink
and white-lace wallpaper walls

*

Our mothers took us to see *The Red Shoes*,
where a woman who had to choose
between love and art danced to death.

But we weren't allowed to see *Pinky*,
a whispered-about movie where a Black
(Negro) woman passed for white.

*

There was a kid my parents knew, with pink
eyes, white hair and skin, and a girl I saw
in a restaurant, with white hair and skin
like the porcelain of a nineteenth-century doll.

*

When white Emily Henderson
is crossed with a blue sweet pea,
purple offspring result. When white
Emily (long pollen grains) is crossed

with white Emily (round), the offspring
is purple, or bicolor red,
a type known as Painted Lady.

*

But in the region   Mississippi
Farabee observed   albino Negroes
taller and broader than   black
We may assume   stature
and breadth   superiority
and if valid   in man evidence
albinization   correlated not
with   but with greater perfection

*

It's everything: the pink
of perfection. To pink is to beautify.

But pink is also something small.
Lift that pinkie. Tickled pink.

And a man in pink is one who hunts,
a pinkish person one who might be red.

*

What if it said race and you had to check pink?
What if white meant only your shirt
or some blankness or parts of your eyes?

Of course you could think pure or spotless or good
but you might need proof. And as for strong,
remember the black leather jacket, the dark suit.

*

maiden   maidenly   meadow   swamp

and one red sock washed it pink

as pink as riven snow

FLOOR STUDY

Sorry, kids, you messed
the exam: it's *err* we trust,

it's *er*, there's no ease in us
anymore, for any user.

And here's Li'l Miss Take
herself, she's crossed a line

she cannot see, a way-
ward vertical line, she says

there is no under under
where we are, just un-

swept dust. And is
that it, the what that bends

the fender, spills the milk,
burns the money, spoils

the work? Why is wrong
our right these days? Thank

you, it was nothing much
the same as nothing more—

In these bare scenes we love
to lose: she gives it up, he shuts

it down, and no one's left
to run the show, which goes

on under cover of some night
before we knew. We're down

to clean-slate work again.
Then it's a question of.

DEER CROW FOX

Fox from woods to woods across
the field, did something happen,
and then the deer making its turn.

Ignore the crows, the flapping,
the caws, *Be quiet* is what
she remembered before she opened

the glass door, then stepped
onto the grass, deer turning
into the colors of the woods.

Small fox, first she'd seen,
cartoon, it went so fast,
brush of a tail, horizontal

as someone's arm, Go and do not
come back. A grown deer, doe,
Well all *right,* she said and went

into the woods, hoping to see
what was there, then fled,
feeling somewhat smaller.

Ignore the crows in the field
with fox, black marks coming
her way, and then the slow-

motion turn of the deer.
But fox first: it starts
in the woods, something must

have happened before the field,
before the crows flew in
from the mirroring sea, and what

did fox mean, streak
of wildness coming out
like that, she kept on coming

back to the place, she would
not let it go this time, this time
she'd get it right, and yet

it's gone, it keeps on being
gone, no arms to bring
it back, no door to open.

IN THE DAYS OF

Once dew leapt over the dome.
A sunning wife yawned

while the naked orb, armed
with odes, aimed at the bay.

But 'nough's enough: the working
title quit, green wheels came

to a slow screech, a first course
in decomposition. End of dash.

Enter, smitten, our regular guy,
shuffling into the war-room, stars

in eyes, tongue in knots.
We're all eyes, but what's

to be seen? It's winks
that wind us up, get us going.

Then a splash of Ohwhynot:
what's a family for, if not for love?

Forget awe, that woozy view,
here's a newer niche where none's

the word: we're what we've got.
Guns in hand, though bombs

are out: there might not be a fire
sale after all, just lots of junk.

Blood etcetera too of course.
Songs about. Including cuts.

Night hovers in hindered measure.
The blunt knee nudges on.

CUTS

A mother holds a girl's legs,
another mother cuts the lips, nips

the tiny bud, she sews, she leaves
a little buttonhole for him

to open up someday, her hands
are washed in blood.

*

. . . the rhythm
of gray, her hand

in her hair,
hand on my hair
as I start to sleep

*

Her mother cannot write the name
she gave her on the envelope.
His mother calls her *her* name.

His sister writes what once was him
and someone else, which someone's
name was his, except for *s*.

*

Be very happy, friends
said. In college they learned

to buy washing machines, to plan
ahead, meat in the oven, knives

on the table an inch from the edge.
Also a little French.

*

. . . her hand
in my hair as I start
to sleep

they're doing it
in hospitals now

sterile knives inch
toward the edge

*

Meanwhile, an airplane's home
from work. It's had a busy

day, it says, what a load, bombs
bombs bombs, but right

on target, boom, and now
it's hungry, fill it up.

*

. . . who rules the roost-
er roaster roast French
hen chickie pie

be very happy, they learned
to write, white words
to buy washing machines, knives
on the button an inch
from the edge

bound in the oven, boots
on the ledge

*

A busy day, an en-
velope, it's his to open, boom
boom boom, her hands
are washed it's
hungry, fill it up.

*

Hold a girl's
legs cut
the lips nip
the bud blood dud

This is the It
Kit and this is Dad
and Mother cannot write
the name he gave her

NOTHING DOING

Dull afternoon, summer sun, it doesn't
have to work/have a clue, a string
bikini'd look great, he said, it must
be fun writing things down. His TV lay
on its side beside the bed, videos under.

Up to her. Into it. A handy hanky, pair
of shorts. Junk, from middle English, old
rope. Oh yes it's, but where oh where?
Bunk beds, pair of beds: on her mind,
or in it? As for X, he came

up short. Pair of shorts. Then
the long feature. She lost interest, as at
the bank. Bled, blurred, a dictionary of.
And what if, if she had to choose. Construction
paper. Yellow slips. Leaves

by the back door. If it's not in this then
what's it in? Listen people are screaming
out there, the street's on fire. What
it's in is what. Something's brewing.
Front burner. Something's up.

OKAY SO WHAT

okay so there was a gun okay so what
okay so he fucked me with it okay okay
okay so there was piss and shit and even
a little blood so what nobody
got herself killed not even
the dog he shot through the window
at and nobody had to eat
the dog to stay alive nobody had
to eat the body nobody cut
the body in half the baby
in half the blood filled nobody's
buckets not even a single
sponge nobody's face got shot
from her face nobody's face
was red because it was nothing
but scars so who did I think I was
to scream those dreams into night
after night his name his face
in my face I didn't even
except in dreams that came after
those dreams I didn't even kill him

CONCRETE MIXER

The clapboard house,
lined like paper. Shadows
on the house, ignoring
the lines. Lines are the cage
of the fan. Writing in air.

Nails in the house, holding
it together. Sharp bonds. And there
they are again, the bodies behind
the door. While under the covers
of school books she was reading . . .

And underneath, when Item A
meets Item B, asks would it like
to dance—? It's very verb.
And then there was grandmother's
microscope. Little bitty fish.

Draw the cat, head-back-tail.
A home-made house, for crying
out loud, with party hats for trees—
O yesterday's bird was a parakeet,
but tomorrow the crows fly home.

He's worth his weight in . . .
Oh, she said. His way to go.
The highway, the dark car.
Concrete: solid, hard.
Gray, between the lines.

LATER THAT DAY

1

*Your mother doesn't see the animals
painted on that wall,* he said. And point-
ing to his I.V. bag and tubes, *Or that
antique, that fine cut glass.*

                    Later
that day, with no one else around, he said,
*You're in cahoots, I know you are, I'm going
out there to get my gun, I'm going to kill
you and throw your rotten body in
the river.*

          Who'd often threatened to kill
himself. Who'd sometimes said *I love
you more than life itself.* Who'd hidden
his Scotch behind the jars of peaches
in the basement. Whose Scotch I found
and finished later that day—

2

                    But *I* could see
the animals there, or anyway I knew
the way the wall breathes a little before
the colors begin to stir, the way the colors
slowly sharpen into form. I could make
that plastic crystal. I could get us out
of that room.

          And I already knew
about the gun, that it aimed both ways
at once, the two-for-one one got by turning
on oneself. I knew how well a gun spoke,
from a drawer in a bedside table as well
as the back of a basement shelf.

                                    The news
was it was him, not someone standing in
for him. The news was it was him
and it was me. Of *course* I was crying.

VALSE TRISTE

Not full but gibbous, she said,
but at least it wasn't square, brown, houses
in little rows, with just a river or two
for diversion, and maybe a single slash
of a road to keep things moving.

And there's our shadow, after all,
down there, where we'd least
expect it, with all that stuff we'd like
to forget. Bodies scrawled on our walks,
broken objects by our doors.

That April, though, she'd danced
in the park among lilacs, and who cared
what might be coming, in little waves.
Walls she'd thought were given
fell in; sky appeared in pieces.

Goodness wasn't an issue, wasn't any-
way to be had: those were the days
they'd drifted, even as others were shot
in the streets, at play or at prayer.
But it wasn't just the guns, the dull rooms.

Let me explain. Touch became
mere friction: even those buttery trumpets
began to grate. And even if
she'd risen, as rise some will in a world
like that, above was nothing more

than occasional light. Better to think
it flat, she thought, surveying the world
she knew. There'd be moments when flags
appeared in unexpected corners. That
would have to do, to round things out.

POINTS

Knife, sword, gun, we meet at some
point or other, yours, you designate, I'm point-
less, zero, blank, having neither length
nor breadth, no part, not even as in hair,
not even hair, no cleft, fold, nothing
there, the way you paint me, sculpt me, draw
a Y of lines to make the point that marks
the us I'm of as *un-*. But there are needles too,
and what's the point but being somewhere one
defines by being there, and when it comes
to finer points, our points are several. Woman
is the third sex, between yours and the one
you make. Zero and one are all the machine
knows. We know better. That's our point.

LINES

Draw a line. Write a line. There.
Stay in line, hold the line, a glance
between the lines is fine but don't
turn corners, cross, cut in, go over
or out, between two points of no
return's a line of flight, between
two points of view's a line of vision.
But a line of thought is rarely
straight, an open line's no party
line, however fine your point.
A line of fire communicates, but drop
your weapons and drop your line,
consider the shortest distance from x
to y, let x be me, let y be you.

LETS

He let her in, he let her out, and then
he let her down. She let him, though, or so
she said, but maybe she was letting on
(remember how she hid that bruise?), let's see
if we can help her out. But then the subject
changed: She let him in, she let him out,
and then she let him down, or did she let
him go? In any case we didn't ask to help
and then we got it. Let x and y
be both believed, let subject I, not sub-
ject to, be listened to, I to I, for all
of us, the ego has no gender. A lease
on life is what we get, *To let*, it says,
a little room, our own, to live and breathe.

LIKES

There was like this guy she said with really
great hair long and blond just like
a girl's you know and I had on this dress
he liked and he had on these running shorts
and shirt which he took off and I took off
the dress which he put on and I put on
the running shorts and shirt I liked the way
they felt like silk against my skin and soon
the shorts were on the floor but not the shirt
my hands were in his hair my hands were like
beneath my dress my hands were his were find-
ing me no her no him no both of us like
he was she and I was he and we and they
were both in both of us two like to like

LIES

Anyone can get it wrong, laying low
when she ought to lie, but is it a lie
for her to say she laid him when we know
he wouldn't lie still long enough to let
her do it? A good lay is not a song,
not anymore; a good lie is something
else: lyrics, lines, what if you say *dear sister*
when you have no sister, what if you say *guns*
when you saw no guns, though you know
they're there? *She laid down her arms; she lay
down, her arms by her sides.* If we don't know,
do we lie if we say? If we don't say, do we lie
down on the job? To arms! in any case,
dear friends. If we must lie, let's not lie around.

RIGHTS

He had no rights, they beat him up, you've got
no right, he said, and he was right, we thought,
we saw them beat him up, right? it happened right
over there, but it was proper form, the jury
said, and they were right, if you could judge
the beating by what happened next, our driver
said, right off they up and burn the place,
this rights stuff goes too far, next thing it's an-
imal rights, vegetable rights, mow 'em down
I say, he said and turned, he had the right
of way, license to get where he needed to go,
but what if they stopped him anyway, they're
the law and that's their right, the right side
of the body's on the other side of the heart.

TIMES

The Times is right, he said at breakfast, time
is on our side. She hoped so; she'd hoped
it all in this good time, finding no place
in the gone-by out-of-mind. Though mornings still
this dark she wasn't sure: did she run against
it now, wind, sand in her face slapping
her down? Or was it, like some lover, running
out on her, not to be seized after all?
Remember the time, she started to say, but knew
he wouldn't, the times they'd shared no longer were
the same. Not that she'd keep time if she could,
not now, after that stunning fall. In no
time: was that what she wanted? Or full
time, one time, her own sweet time of life?

MEANS

But what does it mean, and when does it mean it?
Meaning's mean: somewhere between *What?*
and *Oh!* But meaning's *mean*, I mean look it's only
a means to an *an*. Keep meaning down the street,
you're in no danger. Remember, though, by no
means yes these days. Spell it out, *x*
it *y*, the something under cover/foot's as fat
as its comfy cousin was ere she declined. She meant
well, or well enough, and mean game though
this new kid plays, she's still the means
of support. Mean to mean is one thought. Mean
time the apparent sun sheds light on things.
Apparent things: seeing meaning seeming
things. Marrying means to mean. I mean it. I do.

RACES

The race is on the run, you said. It's not
what it used to be, I said, I mean the whole
question of it, not to mention answers.
Who's ahead, and how, of whom, and who
in the world is whom (sic) to who? It didn't
used to be this way: *race* is something we
made up, and anyway there's nine not three,
and changing all the time. I've only been in one
myself— 5K? And the human one, we're all
in that, but mostly it comes down to two,
and then it's face to face, then arm to arm.
An arms race? A race war? But races run
one way, on one course, to one finish—
even the time you run against is on your side.

SIDES

All you need is two and an angle, a side
is just a line in need of connection, but if
you move a line to the side it's a side,
a side with two sides, front and back, in
and out, depending on what's around (another
story, *around*) to give it depth. Myself,
I'm on the shy side, from my mother's side,
I sleep on my side— I mean it comes from in-
side, we *have* sides, this business of taking
sides. Though how we draw our side lines,
and how we get from opposition's under,
other, out, is less clear. Could we simply
be sides, no angles, right or otherwise,
just siding with, beside, not out or in?

III

LAKE

It's in there somewhere.
It's coming over here, I thought,
as the lake licked the stony shore.

Listen now: a child
playing— no someone dusting
piano keys. Crescendo, diminuendo

of passing boat, passing— above
the still willows passing plane.
Silence. No: cicadas' slow vibrato

fades. Silence. No: hum
in the air, stir in the willows,
waves on the shore, it's coming

over here, I thought, but this
is it, taking it in, click
of a radio—*said the nation*—click

again, sudden sun sheds gold
on wave, illumines the vertical
script of willow, listen,

all attention now,
enter boat, cicada, lake, wade
the waves of sound light mind—

CLOUD-PLAY FOR FOUR HANDS

Let's play clouds.
Let's play *Clouds*.

Let's play, clouds.
Play, clouds, play.

Clouds play.
Could play cloud?

*

Play-clouds roll
when play-clouds play.

Play-cloud's role
in Play-cloud's play
was Cloud.

*

Clouds play for four hands.
CLOUD PLAYS FOR FOUR HANDS!

Cloud-plays for forehands.
Foreplay for cloud and hands.

Three clouds play for four hands.
But four hands play for two.

*

One day a cloud came down to
play. Everywhere it saw hands.
But the hands didn't notice the
cloud.

What could the cloud do? The
cloud was good at play; perhaps
if it just played, the hands
would notice. But the hands
had their own play, and it didn't
include the cloud.

At last the cloud had a thought:
it could play hands! But just as
the cloud was shaping itself into
hands, the hands began to drift
above the cloud.

Good-bye! the cloud-hand cried
as the hand-clouds rose.

*

Hans' hands play
on handy clouds.
Handily Hans
handles clouds.

Hans unhands
cloud after cloud.
Hand over hand
Hans plays clouds.

*

The first one handed down clouds.
The others handed them on.

Clouds in hand,
they plowed clay.

Clouds in place,
they employed hands.

Plan had a hand
in it. Also place.

*

He was an old
hand at play.

My hand, he said,
displaying
his clouds.

He played
into her hands.

IN THE MIST OF ALMOST BLUE

And just when I'd thought of a trip
to Australia, flying out of the clouds,
and that blue reef, they asked and I said

okay I'd do that job, I mean something
to stir things up that were down
to earth and so very cozy. Don't let

yourself get tired, he said, while people
who'd shared a country were killing
each other off, and guns were selling

like ice cream on the streets
of major cities, and then the President
dropped some bombs and everyone said

Ohboyohboy. Ends we lose means no
one wins, but doing's what we set against
undoing—it's how we're made. In the midst

of all that blue is where I'd like
to live, wavy blue floor, floor-to-heaven
blue walls with only a line between, and once,

I'd swear, I did. Now the clouds cloud
that scene, and it's just as well: beyond
the blue horizon's no address in anyone's

book, and besides, there's plenty to keep
us going here at home. To lie back
in those fabulous arms, relax and enjoy

the view, this is your home away
from home, is premature. Up in Adam!
I thought I heard, or was it up

in atoms? But where we live's in time
between: whatever they are, they're what
we're at, so early these late mornings.

MIDDLE

Start in the middle. Stay
there, if you can: up and down
the scale, but always come back to C.

*

Lost in the woods, supposing yourself in the middle
of the woods, you might in fact be very close to the edge.

Where, for that matter, does the middle of the woods begin?

And what about the middle of the story?

*

476-1453: call the Middle
Ages for information.

40-60: the cool or warm
days of middle age.

*

The middle class is the backbone of
this country. The back is the middle
bone of this class. The middle is back
of this country, the country's back
of the class. This bone, this country:

if what you have is a pretty good bone
for your soup, if you can remember
having no soup, if you think *class*
and remember 7th grade, then you might
say *middle* and think *the top* and mean *me*.

*

The middle of
the middle
is the middle.

*

Getting there, he never thought
he'd arrive. He had *places*
to go, he said, *the sky's*
the limit, but come from a three-
room shack with a coal stove,
he needed a roof he couldn't reach
as much as the old linoleum
floor. *More,* he said and said
to his kids. *Stop. That's enough.*

*

In the beginning we're in the middle,
or think we are. We're only on
the edge on the other edge.

*

If you live in the middle of town you don't see the edges.
In the middle of the country you don't see the seas.

If you live in the middle class you miss the others.
If you look in the middle distance you miss the point.

If you find a middle ground you can maybe hold it.
But the middle of the road is a risky place.

*

Above was once our blue
cover, movie screen with lights

at night. Now we think we hold
it up. Weightless, it gets heavy,

while the small hand
of *under* tugs and tugs.

VACANT LOTS

That's it, the gun-shots said,
as someone pitched his pups
in plain sight and the howling began.

Some are many, and angry
as well: at the auction all the tools
were sold, but not the old oak chest.

So why not, then, the tried-true stuff?
Because they said back then that girls
were all like that, when the men

came into the room with their many
names, not to mention the little wife,
and the way everyone fell so easily

into place, under and under. It's true,
when love stayed home the kids
did too, and some of us gave them all

we had in school—if, say, our lover
fell from a boat of a Sunday years
before and never was seen again.

Now the streets hang on the line
like hungry ghosts—scary,
yeah, but at least we can see behind

the proffered arm, the proper knife.
You can take the country out but you
can't put it back in again, you can't

burn all the books, unlearn the words.
If you want to build in spots like these
you've got to use the blocks you've got.

And anyone can play, now the cat's
let out and gone away. None
is altogether, is what's what.

THE LANGUAGE IT WOULD SPEAK

Below, on the off-white surface graphed
with thin gray lines of road and field,
trees are a child's scrawl.

Closer, they say the same one thing,
except in a place where they darken together,
hiding something that has no name.

Descending, I remember things.
The language it would speak, you said.
We have not spoken since.

I spoke because I had to speak.
I, I said, like *tree*, like *plane*,
the thump thump of wheels on the ground.

Once my mother spoke in tongues.
Today she prayed the planes would fly.
My father kept his Scotch in the basement.

They slept in separate rooms and I
have loved mostly in words.
That is what I wanted to say.

That, and *except that night with you*.
It is the It. We are its tongues.
Our tongue is the mother tongue, I said.

That night, your stammering arms
were something older than even that.
My mother waits at the end of the ramp.

You were a new word.

RE: HOUSE(S)

I'm in the doghouse now, he used
to say, and he often was.

But: *Hot* dog! he'd laugh and snap
his fingers and Here-He-Is-Again.

The birdhouse, where Mr. & Mrs. Wren
made their happy home in the tree.

The dollhouse in the bedroom
where parents & children & grandmother

lived with a nurse & a maid & a dog.
Stars on a bedroom ceiling. Things were small!

                        *

So how's
the house?

Hold it, keep
it, paint it

pink, we'll take
it in the morning.

                        *

The house hangs from the ceiling no one can reach it.
There's a safety net but the house could fall through.

A little house with a ladder inside a little house with a ladder
outside you'd have to climb and climb to reach the top.

This is your basic Draw-Houses-Today-Children house: two
straight lines two slanted lines for the roof and maybe a door.

But what do the children draw when they don't have houses.
No door no window no flowers no grass no tree no spiky sun.

On television they had a drawing of STAR WARS drawn by a child.
A big shield over a house and children and flowers a glass dome.

But what if there is no house what if no one can reach it.
What if the net fails if the ladder falls you don't need a dome.

*

You got one I get one two. Too I mean.
Between us two houses. No: *together* two.

Maybe *between*, for cushions, is okay:
to each her own, according to her knees?

At least it's not your usual Let's-Play-House,
Love. At best it's Let's Play Us. And no dog.

*

Mother's moving out of the house. The birdhouse doll-
house doghouse house. It's time to close the door.

Father didn't want to leave. Ever ever ever.
He didn't want to leave to close that door.

*

People are being moved but not as in music
or moving vans or trucks or the arms of friends:

their beds and chairs are piled on the street,
their pots and pans, their pillows and quilt,

boxes tied with flimsy string, a picture slipping
out of its frame, but where is the child who held

that doll, where is the mother who held the child,
where is the father, where are the people who held

these things, a house is meant to be a container,
these things these people can no longer be contained.

*

After awhile, it's all recapitulation:
a house lands on the homeland that was house.

But homeland's where some people come away from.
Homeland's where some people leave a house.

*

What if you live in a tin
house, cold house, no house?

What if you haven't
got a door to close?

CONVEYANCE

We rend, undo, blather still.
Sigh, dear falter, under us.

Darn biography anyway.
Lightsome atoms, warm socks—

Black flaps over the grass
again. A woman with a needle.

At the periodic table we
enjoy our most basic food.

But *un-*'s in hand, our trans-
it token: the beautiful's

the beautiful river, drawing
into itself on its way to the—

O how very afraid he was.
I could've rubbed his feet again.

Elements first! was one of his.
I want to give you some-

thing, he said, *No* I said *I c'n man-
age on my own.* Or held his hand.

The last week, the swallows under
the eaves were gone. Empty unit, used.

He gathered himself, laid down
his beret, releasing an old desire.

O how very. Dumb summer day.
Dust whom light cannot quicken.

FOREST FOR THE TREES

You think trees you think
green. But the weighty
stuff is dark and leaves

are fallen; only needles
color the air, and a few
pale coins of beech. One

large bird disturbed
two afternoons, one
by flight, one by a clumsy

walk. Never to make
another mistake: no crossed-
out lines in the front

of the book, no retraction
in the back, no stammer/blush.
One self-conscious moment,

said my friend, but how
to choose? Heavy
the body, flightless bird, but

see how the earth absorbs
the forest, the water
absorbs the stone.

DISCOURSE

Still night. Still
stars. But the chart
is mechanical, tin turned

in a tipsy circle, the point
of departure is unmarked, the line
of demarcation rusted, smudged.

Okay, so the wished-for one
did not appear. But a letter
came, flew in on wings, and news

is still who knows, a little bird.
And it's not, from morning
egg shells on, all garbage. True,

we aren't climbing stairs or holding
hands, and the signature in the grass
is just grass: we haven't signed.

But once I saw mating skates,
two pliant triangles fluttering
through the waves. Of course

there are many ways, counting
counting. And angles to consider:
between sides, without apparatus

of any sort. *Either* is a side
you could take, you could even
take the underside. But better

not to think of hitting the target.
Better to think of the arrow,
and the bow. There, that's the way.

ACKNOWLEDGMENTS

My thanks to the MacDowell Colony and the Centrum Foundation, where a number of these poems were written, and to the following publications, in which they first appeared:

AGNI: "In the Days of," "Concrete Mixer," "Conveyance"
American Voice: "Likes"
Boston Book Review: "Rights"
Colorado Review: "Re: House(s)"
Crab Orchard Review: "Lines"
FIELD: "Floor Study," "Cuts," "Nothing Doing,""Okay SoWhat," "Later That Day," "Lies," "Sides," "Cloud-Play for Four Hands," "Forest for the Trees," "Discourse"
Graham House Review: "The Language It Would Speak"
Gulf Coast: "In the Mist of Almost Blue"
The Journal: "Valse Triste"
Kenyon Review: "Points," "Lets," "Means"
Orion: "Deer Crow Fox"
Paris Review: "Pinks"
Partisan Review: "Times," "Races"
Prairie Schooner: "Some Things Words Can Do," "Vacant Lots"
The Progressive: "Middle"
The Forgotten Language: Contemporary Poets and Nature, ed. Christopher Merrill (Peregrine Smith, 1991): "Lake"

"Floor Study" appeared in *Pushcart Prize XXI* and "Lies" in *Pushcart Prize XXIII*. A reading of "Rights" is included on the compact disc anthology *One Side of the River: Poets of Cambridge and Somerville* (Say That! Productions, 1997).

"Pinks" was prompted by a statement made by Steve Biko, quoted in *I Write What I Like: A Selection of His Writings* (Harper and Row, 1978) and repeated in the film *Cry Freedom*. "Re: Houses" is indebted to the installation art of Alan Glovsky.

"Pinks" is for Lloyd Schwartz.

A HISTORY OF SMALL LIFE
ON A WINDY PLANET

for Ted

CONTENTS

THE BORDER

Hasta luego and over you go and it's not
serapes, the big sombreros, not even coyotes,
rivers and hills, though that's more like it, towers
with guards, Stop! or we shoot and they do but you don't
need a border for that, a fence will do, a black
boy stuck to its wire like a leaf, a happy gun
in the thick pink hand that wags from the sleeve, even
a street, the other side, a door, a skin, give
me a hand, and she gives him a hand, she gives him both
her hands, the bones of her back are cracking, the string
has snapped, she's falling, she's pleated paper, paper
is spreading and there you are again, over
the edge, you open your hands and what have you got
but confetti and what can you do with confetti, our
side won, a celebration, shaken hands, it matters
now, whatever it is, but how close
you are, your street, the fence behind your house
is the zero border where minus begins, roots
turn branches, cellar is house, you close your busy
mouth to speak, an anti-lamp darkens
the day, and you love that street, its crazy traffic,
you climb that fence, you wave across, there's a rock
in your hand but it's not your fault, you like to travel,
the colorful people, but what if you fell, your house,
your children, the work that gets you up in the morning,
the language gone, the grammar, the rules, the family
talent, those searching eyes, but think of the absence
of eye, a higher tower, a little more wire—
Border? You crossed the border hours ago.

BACKGROUND/INFORMATION

As if a child dialed 411,
asked What is the tallest building
in the world? and a voice replied,

We have no listing.
Blanket statement, he heard
once, and wrapped himself

in the words, as in a canvas
that could wrap itself, edge
painted to edge, body as tube.

—I'm not a real one, I
just play one on TV, which means
I got no parents, education, stuff

like that, not even real trees
(green) or sky (blue) behind me.
Still, we agree: the document says

what it says. And that
was a neat idea, buying guns
with the enemy's money.

Paint the flag on the flag
on the flag, and what do you get,
you get paint. Listen, I'm talking

paint, as in the painter
spent the summer painting
the house, as in 337 Beechwood Lane,

or house, as in white with shutters
and red door. There's a blue sky
in the picture, too, it's a blue

world all over, they say
—but I got a neat idea
that day, I decided to paint a war.

TESTIMONY

There was no paper.
I don't remember seeing the paper.
The paper I saw I don't remember.

Destroying paper is something I do.
There are three good reasons for doing it.
One of the reasons is not forgetting.

Of course I assumed he'd given the orders.
The orders he signed I didn't see.
I don't remember the orders I saw.

The orders I saw have been destroyed.
I don't remember destroying the orders.
They were prepared to be destroyed.

When I saw the orders I ordered the paper.
I ordered the paper to be remembered.
Then I remembered: there was no paper.

BEFORE THE PLANES

Epiphany 1991

We will/we won't they will/they won't
shoot to kill to free to keep

the oil to drive the cars the women
cannot drive across the fields

of sand the fields of grain across
the sea a camel lumbers up

an aisle behind a king a star
of night before the planes the bombs

begin to save the oil to drive you
cannot talk to monsters even angels

have to draw the line the good-
will stuff's for God's guys so God

says so Allah says and the President
bangs his spoon and the President also

bangs his spoon the President says I will
not talk to you I do not like this soup

and the President aims and the President
aims to please to kill to *please* bang bang

COAST

1

Eucalyptus stripping
itself, scenting the air,
a car stops, swallows
its lights, stars blink, open

2

the door of an oriental blue
room, garnet and gold, a room
from the movies, lacking
a wall, or having too much

3

window, flight, a third wing,
below the dark water curves,
an inverse sky, an island
glistens, a constellation

4

of sound, bullets strike
the metal roofs that shine
through banana leaves, the sun
is burning, shrieking

5

children fill the room,
mouths and legs, sexes
bared, nubbin and crease,
bellies rounded, empty

6

baskets to fill with the fruits
of unloved labor, mangoes
hugging their fat seeds, bananas
dangling, grapes spilled

7

from fluttering hands
in the casual blue
Pacific night, arms find
arms in the blank bed.

A HISTORY OF SMALL LIFE ON A WINDY PLANET

First they came in ones
but that was not enough:
they blew away.

Then in twos, hooked together
like scissors, pants, they held
each other down.

But one kept kicking up
its heels, muttering *three,*
unhitching itself,

drifting
into some pair's
pitiful garden.

This went on, you
can imagine: one goes in
to two plus one and three

became the rage but so what?
Say *history* these days
and people sneer:

better the box lunch—
if we eat enough
we'll stay fixed:

nothing, not even love,
can sweep us away.
It's only a matter

of time, after all, dust
in the into and out of
stuff, the girl the wind's loved

since they were kids.
Here's a note, over
the shoulder, under

the desk: It won't
be long. Relax, enjoy.
One's enough. Love—

REMEMBER THE TRAINS?

The friendly caboose. The whistle
at night, the light across the field.

Not a field: her yard,
its little fountain. Not

a fountain: cattle cars crammed
with people. Cattle grazed in the field

of the friendly farmer across the road.
The farmer remembers everything.

She remembers counting the cars,
they were filled with cattle, coal,

it would fall on the tracks. The cattle
cars were crammed, he could see the faces

through the cracks, he could hear them cry
for the water he wasn't supposed to give.

She remembers waving, the engineer
who waved, the tracks behind her house.

He remembers the bodies, he saw them leap
from the windows, he heard the shots,

and the cars returning, empty,
not a whistle, the single light.

The cries she heard were children
at play, friendly children, except the boys

who turned the hose in her face, they said
Come look! she'd almost forgotten.

And the trains kept coming, full,
empty, full again, while the fountain

rose like a flower in the yard that was not
a field and the farmer worked

in the field while they wept,
they waited, they asked for water—

LITTLE BOY

They called the big one Little Boy:
weighed in at five tons, carried

in the belly of a plane named
for the pilot's mother, born, released,

excreted out the back (that old
fantasy), relief, the letting go.

But victory was only the shout
of a child on the street, hurrah

hurrah the generals cried,
the people cried in the missing

city, missing buildings, missing
bodies, missing faces, flesh.

The next one was Fat Man, with more
to come, and now the generals speak

of *wargasm*, everything going off
at once, and what do we say to that?

Because, sometimes, we want to.
Birth is what we're after:

clean plates, table set, the wedding
dress the baby dress the final

satin resting dress and everyone
goes to sleep at the same time—

even the little boy with the pop
gun under his pillow, even the fat

man, all gone, and then we can wake up
and start over again, now can't we.

RUINS

Worn stones, broken walls,
arched, roomed, the pink bones
of a city near a coast.

And a man kept appearing around
the corners, behind the low
walls, was he following her?

In a church in Rome, God
and his mother sit side by side
like lovers, sun and moon

at their bare feet. So history
pulls away from itself, alive
in its dead skin.

And why Rome? The ruins beneath
the ruins, I think. And trouble
all those years ago, that "news."

Keats, of course, but who can say
forever these days, and to whom
do you say it—the nameless

man? the impending child?—
as you walk, a little
too quickly, back to the station.

NEWS OF THE WORLD

The election was won, the game
was lost, but wait a minute, what
about the weather?

Run that by me again,
Mister, the one where the cop
chases the pig— All the way to Maine

they ran, those silly kids,
and meanwhile Mother waited,
tracing lines on a blue map.

Those angry women who stormed
the mall? Now that was something!
But what about the others, gloved?

Listen, there are wars on, all over
the place, here a battle, there
a bomb, and the daisies

are blooming their heads
off, as if there were no tomorrow.
Remember that girl, the home-

coming queen? Shot herself.
Into the phone. Listen,
she said to Minnesota. Then Blam.

But news, shmoos, I read
my books, I play my records, I like
my kids, they're great

kids— It turns, you say.
Yes, I've heard: it's one big move.
Come on, let's get this show

on the road. Wrens moved in
to the wrenhouse today. Someone's
going to die. Someone you know.

HER MOTHER SAID

We heard it at dinner, chicken marsala, rice,
I remember the wine left in the glasses, it
had been in the papers the day before, the mother's
story, her picture, on the daughter's bed,
but our friend knew more than the papers said, knew
why the mother had screamed in court, he couldn't
say but then he did—

                It was after he killed
her, after his hands circled her neck, there,
in the car on the dark road, gun and handcuffs
under the seat, he sodomized her, raped
her the papers said—

               But her mother said, her mother
said the authorities said it wasn't sodomy, wasn't
rape, they said he shoved his fist, his hand
worked and ripped, as if there were some urgent
thing, something he needed up there, to be
got out—

            The organs were never found.
           The evidence was not allowed.
           The body after all was dead.
           Not even the mother got it said
           in court, not even the papers said—

And it's true, it was hard to finish our dinner, hard
to go to sleep that night, and the next day,
from the early plane, Manhattan, phallic, as on
the map, its tip taut with money, hung
suspended, protected between its rivers, as if
it could be detached, got out—

               And then I remembered
a hand in a chicken, my mother's hand, reddish
brown and yellow stuff, and I reached for the bag
on the seat ahead, but there was no bag on that big

jet plane, only a card with exits marked,
and how to use the oxygen mask, first
yourself, and only then your child.

SLUG

Organ adrift in a chipped dish, dime-
store item at garden's edge,
gray glob in golden beer, died
last night, one less to slink
under the leaves of the fattening
squash, eggplant, peppers pushing
the flowers, gray matter, matter
of fact, phallus *without a bone*,
as the panicked mother said, her new-
born's limp, and the sister who cut
her brother's off, stories told
by the wife of the doctor who thrust
his tongue in the young girl's mouth
in the garden behind the rose-
colored house, the softness between
her own small legs gone ashy, dust
of being dead, brain-dead, dead-drunk
at a quarter a mug, slick gray metal
without a face, sliding into the slot.

CLEFT

Cut in half, the breast bone broken, opened,
flattened, flight, if it ever flew,
preserved in the angle of the skinny wings,

and the cleaver raised, *whack*
to the board— A woman wanted to kill
herself, she drew a noose where her name

had been, but last night his fist
came down, across the table she watched
it rise, she watched it fall, as if

for the first time. Then the thud, the glasses
spun, it took her back, an arm rose behind
the frightened child who stood at the window.

Now she remembers the hangman game,
gallows, noose, the man filled in, head,
body, arms, legs, *whack* to the wings, *whack*

to the legs, she could throw the carcass against
the wall, could break the window, climb
on the ledge, letter by letter could spell

her name, the clouds that day, the sharp
bones of the child's small back, wings,
she could fly, she could walk out the kitchen door.

WITNESS

If she says something now he'll say
it's not true if he says it's not true
they'll think it's not true if they think
it's not true it will be nothing new
but for her it will be a weightier
thing it will fill up the space where
he isn't allowed it will open the door
of the room where she's put him
away he will fill up her mind he will fill
up her plate and her glass he will fill up
her shoes and her clothes she will never
forget him he says if she says
something now if she says something ever
he never will let her forget and it's true
for a week for a month but the more
she says *true* and the more he says *not*
the smaller he seems he may fill up
his shoes he may fill up his clothes
the usual spaces he fills but something
is missing whatever they say whatever
they think he is not what he was
and the room in her mind is open she
walks in and out as she pleases she says
what she pleases she says what she means.

PHASE THREE

Driving with her eyes closed,
she thought she remembered a recipe,
a pre-Mesopotamian stew.

I love him to pieces, she'd said
once, of a boy, and later (hand between
her legs as she prayed) of Jesus.

Stop, said the sign. She saw it
at the end of the road, that red
fingerless hand with the white marks.

The word she couldn't say was No.
Maybe, she knew, and Wait a minute,
but much of it was mumbles.

I know, she said, I even knew,
new against the old, she joked,
but when he held her she felt

herself tighten, Yes, she said,
with all she had, with almost all—
No was a bone in her throat.

Out with it, Kidlet, or swallow
it down, she heard,
and remembered the whistling

under the roses: Try this,
if you want to know.
Oh No! she cried, this couldn't

be that, but there it was,
that funny fruit, in her hand.
Well why not, she'd passed

the limit, the angular sun
of the sign said Yield, you had
what you ate—and Honey, it was good.

SLEEP, BABY, SLEEP!

Gotcha! she cried and grabbed a wolf
at the foot of the bed, but it turned

to silk in her hands. Or maybe it wasn't
a wolf: she thought of a woman,

gray, or almost gray, while Mother
was shaking the dreamland tree

and Father was tending sheep,
but have you ever *seen* a ram,

and did you see the cartoon wolf
in the sheepskin coat in the clothing store?

Lambie Pie, her lover would say, and hum
her to sleep, hum hum, she almost forgot

herself, her loss her gain, an I
for a you, but where was her ewe, could he

be she? It rained a lot, the hills
were green, there was plenty to eat,

they were sheep among sheep, but the howls
in the backyard forest, what about them?

The better to love, said the voice
in the clouds, or was it the pillow?

Eat me, the way it says in the book,
the girl in the joke replied.

Then everyone laughed, as everyone will,
those sheep she'd counted falling asleep,

bless Mother and Father, the lambs,
the good gray wolf, oh Love bless you.

THE GOOD GRAY WOLF

Wanted that red, wanted everything tucked inside
that red, that body, it seemed, turned inside out,
that walking flower, petals furled, leaved
by the trees by the forest path, the yellow basket
marking the center—

                           wanted to raise that rose
petal skin to my gray face, barely to brush
that warmth with my cold nose, but I knew she'd cry
for mercy, help, the mother who'd filled the basket
that morning, Wolf, she'd cry, Wolf, and she'd
be right, why should she try to see beyond
the fur, the teeth, the cartoon tongue wet
with anticipation?

                  And so I hid behind
a tree as she passed on the path, then ran, as you know,
to her grandmother's house, but not as they say, I knocked
and when she answered I asked politely for her
advice. And then, I swear, she offered me tea,
her bonnet, an extra gown, she gave me more
than advice, she tucked me into a readied bed,
she smoothed my rough fur, I felt light
as a flower, myself, stamened and stemmed in her
sweet sheets.

                  Not ate her, you see, but rather became
her, flannel chest for the red head, hood
that hid the pearl that when I touched it flushed
and shone. What big eyes! and she opened the cape,
What ears! and she took my head to her heart, teeth,
tongue, mouth to her mouth, and opened everything,
opened me, Woof-woof, she cried, Sweet rose,
I crooned, crawling inside, wolf to flower,
gray to rose, grandmother into child
again, howl to whisper, dagger to cloak,
my mother father animal arms, disarmed
by love, were all she ever dreamed of.

BODIES

A man runs toward me, long
blond hair rising behind
him, penis rising ahead,
as if he ran on a Greek vase,

while a woman circles a tree
with her arm, nipples erect,
someone has trimmed the hair,
you can see the cleft.

Last summer, I wanted to look
inside the body, a body done
with being a body, opened,
to show its parts.

I remembered today, a cardinal
dead at the edge of the yard,
flat as a flower, gutted,
as if for a purpose.

We made love on the beach
that day, and under
the tree, on the edge of the bed.

Something is not enough.

MORE

So what do you want, another
life? Doesn't everyone?
Well I don't know, one

of those beds was just right.
But then she was out on the streets
again. Remember the cats, in Rome?

I get it: you again. This
time, though, the animal hides,
trembling, in the grass.

And just last night we slept
in the barn, naming
the stars, you'd have thought—

A child walks through an empty house.
Almost empty: her mother is in
her bed where she's been for days.

The plate is full. Fist
in the egg, mess in the nest.
You, you, you, all the way home.

CONJUGATION

The Latin teacher wore flowers
with plaids. We knew she'd never marry.

Black and white were concerts
and church, colors that mixed only

on formal occasions. Mother's
answer to What if your daughter—?

was Looks, as in you never
wore purple and red together.

Everything in its place: now and then,
salt and pepper, treble and bass—

In the movies, and in those weddings
where everything matches, we feel better

about ourselves, we feel like Us.
Violets on that blouse, in little bunches.

THEM

They sit in a circle, a semi-
circle, as if onstage, and you
are the audience, watching them beat
their drums in the dim light.

They dance in a circle, a shrinking
circle, their skins glisten, and you
are the victim tied to a stake, the center
they circle, shifting their thick spears.

Of course they do not speak
to you, but they know something you
don't know, a deeper dark you'd like
to know, you in your circle, shrunk

with fear, beating your tiny drum
drum drum (they slink, they crouch,
they huddle, they jump) and what
they know is you, is us: they bear

our weapons, they carry our fears,
another country but distance
is nothing, no one, the country
they are is difference, someone

or other, you or they—curtain
down, house lights on, we sit
in a circle, our hands our drums, we
are center, circumference, everyone.

HOME FIRES

A furnace broke, children disturbed
the neighbors, husbands, wives ran off.

Now they sleep in streets, stations, old
hotels, the children miss their lunch.

The apples are picked and boxed
though the reckoning sheets are torn.

All is forgiven, go home,
he said, the usual smile, and we liked

his little blunders, he was so
a) cuddly   b) cunning   c) cussedly

us, you know, and he always
sent the bad news on a pillow.

But home was where the heart
lurched, A sandwich'll cost

you a sermon, Boy, the Lord
has blessed us richly.

You can't have everything,
he said: two slices of cheese,

please, one then, a little
onion, cabbage, fruit— But the apples

are picked and boxed and shipped.
Rust continues its dull life.

It's the nature of fallen bodies.
Nothing's given. Nothing gives.

EXPOSURE

Exposed roots, pond, swamp, somebody's
been to Mississippi, vines, limbs
dangle, dance, *Where were you, did you ride*
that bus? No, I was young, I had a husband, thoughts
of a child, *And what did you do when they dragged*
that boy from the river, when the killer kissed
his wife for the hungry camera? When my father
was young, five or six, they hung a man,
strung him up at an intersection, *And what*
did you do when they bombed that church, those girls?
When I was ten I made up a friend, a dark-
skinned girl who lived in a swamp, *And where were you,*
leaves on your skirt, when they marched across that bridge?
In the dream I was black, telling myself, who was white,
who I was, like the woman, the soul inside the man,
or the man inside the woman the man who wrote
about these things found hard to handle. *And what*
did you do when they shot—? I marched in the park, arms
linked, with the others. *And did you, ever, yourself—?*
My father, once, he was just eighteen, a kid
dressed in a sheet, *But you?* I didn't, well, a paper
I wrote, I was seventeen, oh the mind's a swamp
with the color drained, like photographs, black
and white, like words on a page, mistakes erased,
And where did you get your evidence? I made
it up, some words I'd heard, the man inside,
a father's words, the girl inside would have
to wait, my made-up love would have to be still,
if she was good like me her time would come.

OWL

Owl leans into the tree and disappears.
A friend disappears down the long concourse,
Palestinian scarf over his thin
shoulders, thin legs, thinned blood,
and we wonder, his former lover and I, how long.

The eyes of owl see better because they cannot
shift, the ears of owl hear better because
they are wide, owl seems wise because of these features,
I learn the day my friend leaves, but we
fear owl: the bird of night by day means death.

The next week, while I'm writing this poem, a notice
arrives that says I'm not to *promote* or *produce*,
and then some words and *homoerotic* and more
words, and I wonder if this could be homoerotic,
a friend embracing a former lover, and could

the disease be homoerotic, could this woman's pen
on this woman's page, snow falling on snow,
hand over hand? Eye to eye, death
on death, could feather on feather on owl's gray back,
check on check on the silky black-and-white scarf?

Like to like, except in sex: to attract
an owl we hooted like owls; to attract a woman
a man may hoot and howl, while the woman coos.
Before he left, my friend let me choose a drawing
from his sketchbook. The woman I chose, nude,

hangs on my wall, while my friend waits and we wait,
everyone waits, day after day, for news—
words travel, in written or silent lines.
Owl makes no sound when he moves at night,
but just before dawn he may answer if you call.

WHEREVER YOU FIND IT

Where do I find Jesus, he asked
the operator. She gave him the number
she'd seen on TV, and now

he's saved in San Francisco,
but listen, Folks, we're in
this soup together.

Last night the car seat burned.
Then the zoo, the bears,
and lastly the kitchen,

and I was afraid.
Love's doing well
in school, they say, but yesterday

he shot his dear, or was it
the man who shot the deer
he shot, he wasn't sure—

You slay me, he said, and slapped
his thigh, and she did,
too, her tongue did, they didn't

like each other much, *each other*
being, understand, themselves,
that Thursday trash.

A hearty stew, someone said,
but that had nothing to do
with the hearts and minds

of this generation. They met
in that Jacuzzi store, her limbs
(she called them limbs) were sore—

O my people, rise from your beds
of ashes, feathers, beat
those swords, and Lady,

put that anger away!
But she needed all she could get.
She needed you.

LAST THINGS

Cows' hooves crack, crows
gather, a hard winter

is coming, sure as the Lord, fire
on the plains, bones snap

underfoot in the snow, walking
on bones the spine rises up

up-up! through the clouds that whiten
the sky where the Lord is waiting

with fire in His mouth, take that
and that and you will, oh yes,

you're dancing on ice, the sweep
of the blade, you're climbing

the bank to the little wood hut,
you're warming your hands

by the fat coal stove, there's fire
in the belly, fire on ice! a marvelous

drink, says the lady in red, her hands
are bones, her flesh is a dress,

a transparent dress, you have seen
the bones that wait

by the sink, you can suck
them out, there are worms

in the house, an owl cries out
like a woman on fire, roots

push deeper, cling to the soil but
winter has come, white flames

are falling like snow and nothing
will ever be born or cold or dead again.

AFTER

After the scattering, after the nights of shattered
glass, broken stones, scrawls, marked
houses, chalked walls, after the counter
threats, shouts, shots against the scattered
unhoused stones, after the bombs from over
the ocean, the desert, after oil has mixed
with blood, after the blossoming desert is bombed
to sand and risen again to blossom, though this
is more than the story tells, the story, simply
begun with the scattering, ends with the gathering
in again from distant cities, countries, corners,
basements, caves where children were hidden, graves
whose bones were moved to be burned, ashes that would
not burn, from earth, from air, the people will come
together, they will ride in carts and trains
and cars, they will walk and run, and this
is the story, the people will cross the oceans,
they will cross the rivers on bridges made
of paper, blank and inked and printed and painted
paper bridges will bring them together, over
the waters the borders the wars will be over, under
the paper bridges that bridge the most the best we can.

MYSTERY RIDES

1

Mystery rides the train to work.
Gabriel plants stones.

They draw together
on the living room floor—

2

Mystery lines the way to work.
Gabriel slants bones.

They gnaw together.

3

Who does Gabriel think he is,
tooting that little horn?

4

Mystery likes the way the world
turns on its little stem.

5

Gabriel's still in the backyard, Mom.
He's digging those funny holes again.

Gabriel's an angel, Sweetie.
Angels are different from us.

6

Mystery slips through the thick rain
in the living room train. He sleeps
alone, he slides in slips in sleep.

7

Gabriel, that kid who goes
to nursery school, draws pictures
of stones and stuff.

I was thinking someone—
you know, grown.

8

Mr. E. drives his white car
through the gray rain.
He is going to work.

He hums a rainy tune.

9

Mystery hums a single word.
Gabriel holds the phone.

10

This morning I drove my car
to work, stones in my throat,
I opened my mouth and a song
came out, in the mirror a white car—

11

Mystery hides where Gabriel lurks.
Gabriel slips in.

They draw together.

12

Mystery man, with a kid
inside: the angel
angle. Vibrant stones.

Mister Angel, is that you?

HAMMERS

A woman who all year has drifted
toward rage—testy, she heard
someone say—or not really rage,
she has merely held in,
held back, her fingers locked, her eyes
on guard, her heart ready to pounce
on a morning Hello, sits at a piano.

A man smiles, and she places
her fingers over the keys, hammers,
her teacher once said, and she tests
them, tap tap tap, tap tap,
she thinks of Chopin dying, and dying
more quickly because of the rain
on a house on Majorca, the rain

of the Preludes, her teacher said,
and she knows it's not true, but she liked
her teacher for saying it was, a house
on Majorca, a man and a woman alone
in the right hand, the left the rain,
steady and strange, hammers, he said,
as her fingers tapped through the rain.

Oh play! says the man, and she thinks
she's forgotten, but then her hands,
as if there were strings, rise
and come down on the patter of notes,
falling as if on a house on Majorca,
rain drizzles down and the man
starts to sing, she's never heard him

sing before, la la la la la la, he sings,
a lusty baritone la! and she plays,
she plays, it's been years but her fingers
are hammers striking the keys that strike
the hammers inside the piano, la la
la la, the right and the left, a man
and a woman are building a house in the rain.

LOVE LETTUCE

The Boston lettuce sprawled
in its bed, it wouldn't come to a head.

But the flowers were working,
their little systems of he and she,

pistils poised, anthers moving in
for the kill— Kill? Who said Kill?

Love, let us be true, he said,
eighteen inches between the plants,

love, lettuce, beet, rue, she kept
tending the garden, minding the roots.

Meanwhile the sea moved
as in sex, though it has no sex,

*If I had to draw a picture
of God, I would draw the sea,*

*if I had to say I would call it she,
her absolute arms, her better than good*

enough love, she said. Then he snipped
the ribbon that held her hair and tied

her wrists, no he tied a line
between two stakes, but she felt a tug,

the unlined sea pulled out, his arms
drew in. *C'mon, now, remember*

*the rules: seeds fall and trees rise
and beach grass holds the shifting*

*sands, eighteen inches, love
your dad, mind your manners, don't—*

She held a daisy against her breast.
How do you spell unh-uh? she asked,

but just then the ground swelled, oh
yes, the stakes fell, and the rocking sea

of love, where one still throbs inside
another, also throbbing, rose to meet them.

TREE

Tree tree tree tree leaf tree tree tree
leaf hand leaf hand oak leaf oh
tree oval leaf eye leaf mouth leaf oh
tree trunk tree uh-oh try tee
tea two too tutu mush dog
sled horse cart model T cruising
down the high way road bed *uh-*
oh teed on treed off the track
again retract am track not
train *T* (rah!) *R* (raw) *A*
e i no t just rain rein hands and
the mockingbird singing in thee
elum tree like to the something
heavenly o u o me-oh-my oh you oh my-o

FIELD

The window fell out the window
and having only a frame
to refer to, we entered

a new field, the space filled
with lightness, wheat field, sweet
field, field of vision, field

and ground, and the puzzle became
the principle, a page without
a single tree, but you kept coming

back to the place, your fingers
reading my skin, and I cried Love!
before I could stop myself, love

is a yellow shirt, light
is what it thinks when it thinks
of itself, and now it shines

through both our skins, in
the field, out of the field,
two in the field where none

had been, field to field
with particles stirred
into being where we touch.

DOWN THE ROAD

You think Food and you're fed.
You think Sleep and you disappear.
You wake and you're everywhere.

Then someone points *You, there,*
and off you go, in your yellow
slicker and red rubber boots,

down the road but do not cross,
do not go past Susan's house, do not
talk to strangers, feed the dog.

Just this morning sun filled
my scrunched nose, snow was good
to eat, I ran ahead.

But *road* is already down
the road, two-car dream, house
machine, on/off is what it knows,

and down the road the road ends
at another road, in a field,
in mid-air, the freeway years

ago in California, or this year,
when the road fell on the road.
Love your country, go to church,

but down the road the road ends
are tied in a knot that only
a child can undo. That's

where you come in, you
of the *everywhere*, but also
you of the here and there,

eating crumbs that lead
to the table, coiling string
on your fingers, keeping time.

I slept over at Susan's house.
I slept over again but now I wake
in the nimble shadow that is

your arms and there we are.
The car starts, we're in it,
but only the road is passing by.

MASS

It starts when a boy, or someone
who seems to be a boy, walks out
of a building, into the unexpected
rain, and crumples a paper into
his jacket, jostling the keys to his
father's house, and starts to think
of wet clothes, but rain is streaking
the air at a visible slant, like light
on water, like something that doesn't
quite, how can he say it, fall
as it falls, not like a baseball that arcs
through the air, but something that
buoys him up, and he dashes
into the rain, the rain is the road
that carries his racing feet, and racing
he knows the body he is, not weight
exactly, but something that will not
without an effort be moved
or stopped, like the day he slid
into second base, no it isn't
weight, he imagines a body floating
in space, the way the aquarium
turtles float, heavy and huge, but not
even that, rather something that isn't
a body at all, that comes from body, is born
from body, a little perhaps like the baby
he was, except this would happen
like light, a shower, explosion
of light that would start with something
the size of a baseball, and then
begin splitting, releasing, splitting,
releasing and something that is
wouldn't be, his father says
the earth could die, but say he
died, his merest self, say his body
itself released itself, let itself rise
through the slanting rain, it leaps
and it rises, climbing the air, the slant

of the rain, it is not a boy, there are
no bases, no fields, there is only
everywhere rain, bless father, bless
mother but he is rising, the keys
in his pocket, the uncrumpled paper,
the rain a cable of light beginning and
ending nowhere but rising and being now.

WRAPPED

Sweater, jacket, patchwork quilt, chair
by the fire, a country room in early spring—

Dead limbs unwrap themselves, birch
paper pulled away in winter, spring

leaves unwrap their small green selves, cocoons
wrap wings, their swaddling shrouds, and it

was wrapped in smooth white paper, square
box, a birthday gift, someone tucked, folded,

taped, and someone put it in the ground,
wrapped and wrapped the unwrapped burned-up body.

You can play cabbage on the piano. Also
baggage. Bed and bad and dad and dead.

For weeks he shed his solid flesh, bones
ridged his limbs, his face, he tossed, he prayed,

he turned, he raged, he didn't like the white
room, he didn't want to die, to live,

but once when Swan Lake played on the tape,
his thin arm rose from the white bed, dancers

leapt across the room, sheets untucked
themselves, took flight, long white necks stretched

through the window, Yes, he said as he laid down
his baton, as he laid his arm by his side to sleep.

You can't play God, you can't play good.
But you can feed a babe, face the dead.

He couldn't stand. A hand on his shoulder steadied
him, but he slid from his chair, slid to the floor

where a fire burned in a coal stove and a young
man straightened his first tie and the tie

unwound to a boy in a wagon, cap on his head, dog
by his side, to a boy playing ball in a sailor suit,

to before-the-boy in a long white dress, same
brown eyes, baby bones wrapped in fat, wrapped

in arms, till the arms release, undo, undress,
and he's back inside, wrapped in water, bliss.

The funeral march is a children's chant:
dum-dum-dum, he is dumb-and-done-and-gone.

Dear flesh that held me, arms, lips, *This*
could be a better world, dear words, thoughts,

senses gone, ashes boxed beneath a tree,
but his arm rose as he laid him down, back

he swam, cell by cell, fingers, toes,
limb buds gone, a better world, head

knot, tail, two cells, one, a single world,
unwrapped of flesh, splitting, thought, wrapped

in flames, wrapped in God, dear shoulder,
father, ashes in the warming, swaddling ground.

THE SCRIBE, DISTRACTED FROM HER LABORS

The letters grow on the page,
I think, and somewhere deep
in the reaches of some tree's branches
is every one, the story's
every letter, even the last O can be found
curving into itself in the afternoon light.

How sweet the light
falling upon this page
I thought this afternoon and found
myself writing it into the text, deep
in a sentence, walking into the story.
The light shone through the branches

outside the window onto the branches
I wrote, drawing me in, that delicate light,
until I couldn't tell story
from scribe, text from page,
outside from in, oh I was deep
in it, going deeper, and what I found

at the bottom was that day I found
the road from town, the branch
to the right, but I turned left, deep
through the trees, following only the light
of a muttered message. This is a page
from another story,

it's not the story
I meant to tell— What I found,
what brought me here, was not the page
the abbess cited, vine and the branches
we're meant to be, but the one with the light
that was God and the word so deeply

word it was light: deep,
I felt myself sinking, into that story,
wanting nothing except that light
slicing the darkness I'd found
that afternoon we lay on the branches
we'd spread. That's another page

of that day's story. This is what I found
today: the light I sought on the page is the same light
that fell on those branches. It's that deep.

ACKNOWLEDGMENTS

A History of Small Life on a Windy Planet was first published by the University of Georgia Press in 1993. Individual poems first appeared in *AGNI*, *American Voice*, *Boston Phoenix*, *Denver Quarterly*, *FIELD*, *Kenyon Review*, *New Directions 55*, *Partisan Review*, *Ploughshares*, *Poetry East*, *Prairie Schooner*, *Southern Review*, and *West Branch*.

The collection was supported by grants from the National Endowment for the Arts and the Ingram Merrill Foundation; by the Poetry Society of America's Alice Fay Di Castagnola Award; and by the MacDowell Colony, where many of the poems were written.

"Remember the Trains" was influenced by Claude Lanzmann's film *Shoah*, which is the source of the final line and a half of the poem. "The Good Gray Wolf" is indebted to Amanda Claiborne, "After" to Rudolf Baranik's memory of a Yiddish folksong, and "The Scribe, Distracted from Her Labors" to Mary Shaner's account of a scribe's interpolation into the manuscript he or she was copying, quoted here as lines 7 and 8 of the poem.

"Owl" is in memory of James Fudge.

"Down the Road" is for Paula Rankin.

BIOGRAPHICAL NOTE

Martha Collins's other volumes of poems include *The Arrangement of Space* (1991) and *The Catastrophe of Rainbows* (1985). The recipient of many awards, including fellowships from the NEA, the Ingram Merrill Foundation, and the Bunting Institute, Collins has also co-translated, with the author, *The Women Carry River Water* (1997), a collection of poems by Vietnamese poet Nguyen Quang Thieu. She founded the creative writing program at the University of Massachusetts-Boston, and recently began co-directing the creative writing program at Oberlin College, where she is also serving as an editor of *FIELD*.